A MAN AND HIS MISSION
Cardinal Léger in Africa

"I am only one man, one part of humanity."

A MAN AND

HIS MISSION
Cardinal Léger in Africa

KEN BELL

text by HENRIETTE MAJOR
translation by Jane Springer

PRENTICE-HALL OF CANADA, LTD. SCARBOROUGH, ONTARIO

Canadian Cataloguing in Publication Data

Bell, George Kenneth, 1914-
   A man and his mission

Issued also in French under title: Un homme et sa mission.
ISBN 0-13-548115-5

1. Léger, Paul-Émile, 1904-   2. Missions to lepers —
   Cameroon — Pictorial works.
I. Major, Henriette, 1933-   II. Title.
BX4705.L45B4513   282'.092'4   C76-017086-X

© 1976 by PRENTICE-HALL OF CANADA, Ltd.,
Scarborough, Ontario. Published simultaneously in the
French language under the title "Un homme et sa
mission: le cardinal Léger en Afrique" by Les Éditions de
l'Homme Ltée, 955, rue Amherst, Montréal, Québec.

Prentice-Hall, Inc., Englewood Cliffs, New Jersey
Prentice-Hall International, Inc., London
Prentice-Hall of Australia, Pty., Ltd., Sydney
Prentice-Hall of India Pvt., Ltd., New Delhi
Prentice-Hall of Japan, Inc., Tokyo
Prentice-Hall of Southeast Asia (PTE.) Ltd., Singapore

ISBN 0-13-548115-5

Design/Julian Cleva

1 2 3 4 5 80 79 78 77 76

Printed and bound in Canada

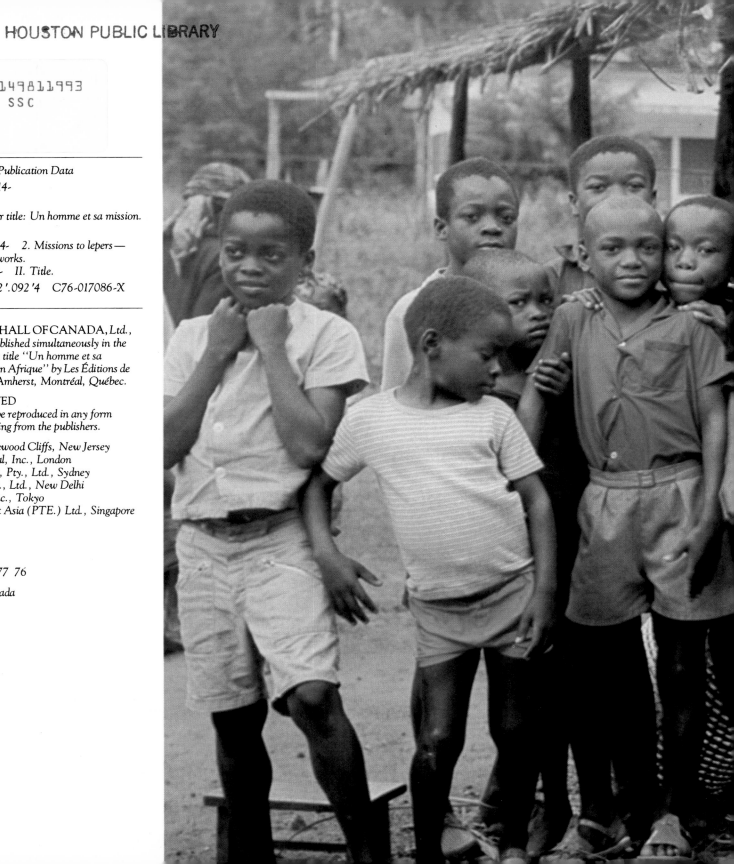

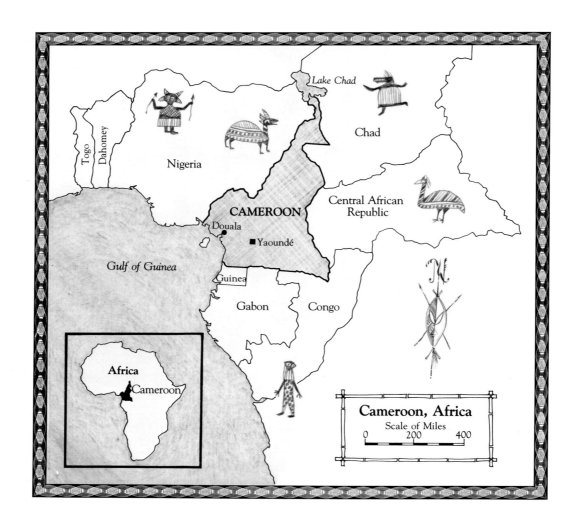

Togo

Dahomey

Nigeria

Lake Chad

Chad

CAMEROON

Douala

■Yaoundé

Central African
Republic

Gulf of Guinea

Guinea

Gabon

Congo

Africa

Cameroon

Cameroon, Africa

Scale of Miles

0   200   400

Contents

Message from the President of Cameroon
Dedication by Paul Emile Cardinal Léger
Foreword by Jean Zoa, Archbishop of Yaoundé

Message from the President of Cameroon

Paul Emile Cardinal Léger deserves our admiration and gratitude for his magnificent work in aid of the handicapped of Cameroon.

AHMADOU AHIDJO

Dedication by Paul Emile Cardinal Léger

From the very beginning of the two projects which enabled me to provide substantial aid to the lepers and the handicapped children of Africa, I appealed for the active cooperation of many lay people. The success of these works is due in great part to their initiative. To name them all would fill many pages of this book, but I will make an exception to underline the devotion of former and present chairmen of the projects. Bernard Benoit deserves special mention. For many years he was chairman of both the movement for the lepers, "Fame Pereo", and the project for handicapped children. Our Lord called him to a more perfect service; in taking his religious vows at the abbey of St. Benoit du Lac, he consecrated the rest of his life to the praise of God. If you read these words, dear Brother Bernard, find in them proof of my eternal gratitude, which you share with your colleagues and especially with your daughter, Francine...

The successors to the chairmanship of Bernard Benoit still manage our affairs. Maurice Gravel and his board of directors are busy overseeing the work for lepers. Marcel Vincent and his colleagues follow the progress of "Cardinal Léger and His Endeavours" very closely.

I would be remiss if I did not express my gratitude to Father Robert Riendeau, whose untiring devotion helped overcome many difficulties in the African work.

This book, which is also an album of memories, is dedicated to the thousands of donors who have supported my work over the last ten years. Some of them have contributed enormous amounts of money. Many have given the small coins of the poor, which before God are just as precious.

+ P.E. Card Léger   PAUL EMILE CARDINAL LÉGER

Foreword by Jean Zoa, Archbishop of Yaoundé

The affection between His Eminence and myself grew out of what I would happily call a "Counciliatory friendship". I will always remember this Cardinal who came so early into the Council hall to say his rosary or prepare his speeches. It was in this way that we had time to work together on the development and the focus of LUMEN GENTIUM, GAUDIUM et SPES, AD GENTES* —and that was how we got to know each other.

A year after the Ecumenical Council, I was invited by His Eminence to give the sacrament of confirmation to hundreds of young Québecois in the parishes of Montreal. It was at the end of that year, on December 27, 1967, that Cardinal Léger arrived in Yaoundé.

From the time of his first contact with the press in Yaoundé, the Cardinal made it very clear that: "I have not come with a specific project in mind; I have come to put myself at the disposition of the poor people and the Church and the authorities of your country". This attitude of humility and readiness to serve, far from diminishing, continued to grow stronger.

The Cardinal was known in Africa for his interest in the lepers, those afflicted by the "biblical illness", and this issue is the one raised almost exclusively by the international press: the Cardinal left his position to devote himself to the lepers.

Because of his respect for the wishes of the local government and Church authorities, the Cardinal agreed not to let himself be

*The documents of the Council on the Dogmatic Constitution on the Church, the Church in the Modern World, and the Church's Missionary Activities.

monopolized by the lepers, and extended his interest to all areas which had been designated "urgent" or "top priority". The list of his accomplishments shows very well the universal scope of his feelings and interests.

I will always remember the lengthy pilgrimage that we made to all the authorities and health services in order to find out their precise objectives and to ensure that none of our efforts would conflict with theirs. We visited the Ministry of Health and Social Welfare, the Prime Minister's office, the Central Hospital, the Jamot Centre, the Epidemic Services, etc., etc. It was after these discussions that the Cardinal agreed to build the Centre for the Rehabilitation of the Handicapped. The Cardinal devoted himself to the project wholeheartedly. He was sixty-three when he arrived, but you would have thought him forty — visiting dispensaries, staying in leprosaria. . . . In one year the Cardinal gave the sacrament of confirmation to all of the fifty-eight parishes of the Archdiocese.

From the first day, Cardinal Léger liked to say that being a Cardinal was an encumbrance. I must say that it never seemed so to me. His simplicity of manner puts people at ease; his good humor and his attentiveness to others made us forget that he was a Cardinal.

This attentiveness to people and to local problems went hand in hand with a deep concern for the problems, struggles, and anguish of the universal Church and of all humanity. Nothing happened in the Church or in the world which did not have immediate repercussions for him and for his work.

When visitors to Cameroon saw the Centre for the Rehabilitation of the Handicapped they sometimes exclaimed: "Couldn't you have done something else? Is this really a priority?".

As I pointed out above, when the Cardinal arrived in Cameroon he had no intention of creating a rehabilitation centre for handicapped

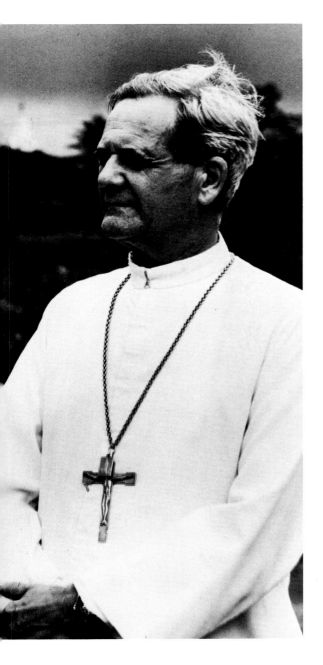

children; it was the Cameroonians who converted him to this idea because the need for such a centre had been strongly felt. They wanted to go ahead with the project because of its essentially human nature.

Anyone traveling through the bush of Cameroon at that time was struck by the sight of thousands of human beings living in misery and neglect. The handicapped were considered a kind of curse, an indication of the presence of an evil spirit and bad blood in the family. In view of this attitude, there's no need to mention the helplessness of the parents and the family as a whole. The rehabilitation project, for these Cameroonians, was first of all an affirmation of the intrinsic worth of every human being. Thus it gave a glimmer of hope to all of these families; it was a kind of collective exorcism which liberated both the children and the family.

To those who see everything in economic terms, this work seemed to be a waste of money; but in view of the increasing dehumanization of our large African cities, the presence of the Centre is a reminder of values more important than those which usually preoccupy us — money, status, and power . . .

Finally, I would like to mention the characteristics of the Cardinal which made the deepest impression on me: his tactfulness and his humility. I wish all the pastors in the world could have assistant priests as dynamic, as cooperative and as compliant as Cardinal Léger was with me.

In thinking of the Cardinal's presence and work among us, many Cameroonians say to themselves: "The Vatican II Council was really very important!" Others add: "The saints exist, even now."

+ yloa
JEAN ZOA
ARCHBISHOP OF YAOUNDÉ
Yaoundé, February 27, 1976

THE MAN

"INASMUCH AS YE have done it unto one of the least of these, my brethren, ye have done it unto me." These words from the Gospel seem to have inspired the life of His Eminence, Paul Emile Cardinal Léger, the man the people of Quebec still affectionately call "le Cardinal".

In November 1967 Cardinal Léger announced his decision to resign as Archbishop of Montreal to become a simple missionary in faraway Africa. His decision was the first of its kind in the Catholic Church and it stunned not only the people of Quebec but the whole world. He had been Archbishop of Montreal since 1950 and Cardinal since 1953. A dynamic man, he had exerted a strong personal influence on the position and on all with whom he came in contact. He was a familiar figure in his scarlet robes of office, serene and gracious, loved and respected by his people, who responded spontaneously to his frequent appeals, even then, on behalf of the underprivileged. Little by little they accepted the new image of the Cardinal, an aging man dressed in a simple white cassock, moving amongst the lepers of Africa, working with handicapped children, the sick, and the starving. The Cardinal never got used to the misery of others: "The Lord had pity on sinners, but he was also interested in relieving physical suffering," he said. Through the prestige earned during his years of service, he hoped to be able to direct some of the resources of the rich to the unfortunate of Africa and so relieve some of the suffering.

At age seventy-two, when he could be living in the peace of retirement, he continues to work to maintain and develop his African projects. Back in Canada since February 1973, he still endures exhausting trips to Africa in order to boost the morale of his workers. However, now that his work in Africa is well-established, he realizes that he is more useful in Montreal, where he and a small team continue to solicit

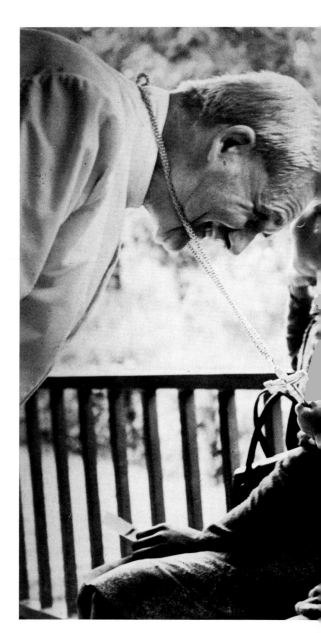

the aid which is so essential to the continuation and growth of these projects.

Yet it is in Africa that he is most content—as ascetic amidst the rich green landscape. His features, marked by age, work, and many worries, brighten suddenly with a smile that betrays an incredible youthfulness as he circulates among the children, embracing one, encouraging another, taking the smallest into his arms, amused as they play with the cross around his neck. In the chapel, he speaks seriously to the children in simple terms about the meaning of suffering and the joy of living despite their handicaps.

By what strange path did this man come to a life of active benevolence in a country where nothing would seem to attract him? In order to understand something of this evolution, it is necessary to trace the exceptional career of the Cardinal and to follow the ways of Providence in his life.

THE FUTURE CARDINAL was fascinated by the men who gathered around the stove in the evenings to discuss politics in his father's general store in Saint-Anicet, a small village not far from Valleyfield, Quebec. It was through these conversations that young Paul Emile began to understand the outside world; this small society was a microcosm of the larger one in which he already dreamed of playing a role. He quickly completed his primary studies at the village school; in those one-room schoolhouses bright children soon learned to assimilate the teaching intended for the more advanced grades. He was an altar boy and often served Mass, doing so with piety. His favorite game was to imitate the priests saying Mass, and in this he was encouraged by his maternal grandmother, a very religious, even mystical woman. At the age of twelve, the boy was sent to the Junior Seminary of Saint Thérèse on the advice of his parish priest, who had studied there. "In those days, it took me two days to travel from my home to the college," the Cardinal explains, "and nowadays it takes me only one day from Montreal to Yaoundé, the capital of Cameroon!"

Already young Paul Emile dreamed of entering the priesthood. Unfortunately, after his second year of secondary school, sickness forced him to interrupt his studies. He speaks of the three years which followed as "the painful years". In addition to his health problems, the young man also suffered from loneliness, as his parents had moved to Lancaster, a small town in Ontario. He tried working at a number of different jobs, such as electrician, mechanic, and butcher. Early Christmas morning in 1923, after receiving communion during the Midnight Mass, he went to meditate alone in the choir loft. "I remember it as if it were yesterday," says the Cardinal. "I heard a voice say to me very firmly: 'You will become a priest'." This was a decisive moment in his life. He completed the secondary course and entered the Grand Seminary in Montreal. "I've never been sick since," he says, "I devoted myself to the

(Above) *Childhood home.* (Right) *The chancel of the Church of St. Anicet*

(Above) *St. Cecile Cathedral in Valleyfield*
(Left) *Church of St. Anicet*

studies which were to lead me to the priesthood. I loved the atmosphere of the Grand Seminary."

He was ordained in May 1929, and set off for Paris that September. He had decided to join the Sulpicians and he spent his novitiate at Issy-les-Moulineaux. "The day I arrived, he says, "two Sulpicians were leaving for the mission at Hanoi. This coincidence awakened in me an old desire to become a missionary." After finishing studies in canon law, he taught for two years at the seminary of Issy-les-Moulineaux. Then, during a vacation in Canada, he learned that his superiors had chosen him to establish a seminary at Fukuoka in Japan; his dream of a faraway mission was realized. He worked in Japan from 1933 to 1939 and in this troubled period before the war, he learned how difficult the beginnings of a new project can be.

In 1940, international events forced him to return to Canada where he was named vicar general of the diocese of Valleyfield and pastor of the cathedral. The seven years he spent there were active and rewarding: "I lived in a fervent Christian community." In spite of his love for teaching, the Cardinal was immediately at ease in the role of pastor. "Preaching is another form of teaching," he says. Besides, he says that speaking has always been his favorite form of expression. In his leisure time, he gave lectures at various institutions, his favorite subject being "Claudel, the Christian Poet".

This vigorous young priest was often chosen for the most difficult tasks. The Canadian College in Rome had been occupied during the war years by the Italian army, and the building had become dilapidated. It was the future Cardinal who was chosen to restore and reorganize this prestigious college. Struck by the misery which existed in most of Europe during the post-war years, he organized fund-raising campaigns in Quebec to purchase such necessities as powdered milk, cod-liver oil and clothing. In one year he distributed 4,000 cases of goods to the needy in

25

(Above and Right) *Mary, Queen of the World Cathedral in Montreal*

27

Rome. Already he was showing his concern about the uneven distribution of wealth.

In 1950, when he was forty-six, Paul Emile Léger was appointed Archbishop of Montreal. Three years later, he was promoted to the rank of Cardinal, the youngest prince of the church of his time. The "p'tit gars de Saint-Anicet" rose quickly through the ecclesiastical hierarchy and during the next seventeen years played an influential role in Quebec society.

During his years in Montreal, Cardinal Léger waged a merciless fight against poverty. "The battle against poverty won't be won until its existence becomes intolerable to the entire population," he declared at the beginning of his term. He founded two refuges for the homeless in Montreal, the "Foyer de la charité" and the "Port du ciel". Then, thanks to an appeal which was responded to by all sectors of society, he restored an old building which became the Saint Charles Borromée hospital for the chronically ill. The famous "corvée du Cardinal" brought together workers from all trades who willingly gave a few hours for the "Cardinal's hospital". No one had ever seen anything like it; the Cardinal had succeeded in convincing people that poverty is everyone's concern.

At the same time as he was trying to relieve the misery at home, the Cardinal concerned himself with underdeveloped countries. "We have erected a wall of egoism and indifference between us and the people who suffer. Overfed Canadians hide behind their piles of wheat while two thirds of the world's population are dying of hunger," he stated bitterly to the members of the Montreal Chamber of Commerce in 1962. The Cardinal described this imbalance as the "collective sin that the well-fed commit in complete disregard of justice and humanity."

Quesnel House (1780) in Lachine, where the Cardinal often received guests when he was Archbishop of Montreal.

At the Ecumenical Council of 1963, Léger was one of the most outspoken leaders in the discussion of the decree on religious freedom and one of the architects of the decree on ecumenism. These preoccupations anticipated the time when he would exchange the scarlet cardinal's robes for the white cassock of the missionary. "The bishop must serve—not be served," he declared at the Council. "I would like to see a more modest use of insignia, clothes, and titles in the high ecclesiastical positions." According to him, the use of the old pageantry was an obstacle to evangelical efforts for the poor.

THE MISSION

IN DECEMBER 1963 Cardinal Léger visited the Canadian missions in Africa. This direct contact with the destitution and suffering of the African people troubled him and forced him to question what he might do. An enormous sense of pity overwhelmed him: "It was clear that Our Lord was asking me for actions as well as words," he said in explaining his resignation as Archbishop of Montreal a few years later. On one hand were the world problems of hunger, illiteracy, and under-development; on the other, our technocratic civilization centered on efficiency to the detriment of human values. The Cardinal had made his choice. After the Synod of 1967, he left both his comfortable way of life and the honors of his position to consecrate his body and soul to the destitute. During the next eight years, the Cardinal spent most of his time in Africa, devoting his talents as organizer and administrator to the service of Africans.

The first contact with black Africa is a shock to North Americans used to comfort and abundance, especially if they avoid the big hotels and the usual tourist routes. Most of the time beautiful paved highways, big department stores, and high standards of hygiene must be forgotten; running water and electricity are the prerogatives of the rich, who live in concrete houses and who are, for the most part, Europeans or other whites. Outside the cities, the majority of blacks live in small huts, tiny structures of bamboo covered with clay. The roofs, especially in the bush, are thatched with palm or banana leaves. In the villages, one sees here and there the occasional luxury of a corrugated tin roof.

Men, women, children and old people crowd around the huts, and one wonders how so many people can live in such limited space. The number of beggars and sick people is astonishing; the Africans don't send their handicapped to institutions. It's easy to understand, in view of the great needs, why the Cardinal chose Africa as a field of action. "The

(Above) *A village family.* (Left) *The cacao harvest*

adaptation has been slow; everything can't be done in a day. My years in Africa, with their constant worries, have been very tiring. At times I feel very weary."

(Above) *Sister Lise Carignan, nurse at Nsimalen, with Father Bouchard in the background*

AT THE TIME of his rounds of the African missions in 1963, the Cardinal was very distressed by the leper colonies. The living conditions of these people seemed to him particularly painful. On his return from the Council, he founded the Fame Pereo movement ("I am dying of hunger") whose purpose was to gather funds for the care of lepers. But it wasn't sufficient for the Cardinal to give only money; he wanted to give of himself as well. So in 1967 when he decided to live in Africa, he thought at first of working with the lepers. He spent six months in a colony of 300 lepers at Bafia in Cameroon. "You have to live with the lepers to understand their suffering," the Cardinal affirmed. The house he built at Bafia is now part of the hospital.

At the Council, he had become a friend of Jean Zoa, the bishop of Yaoundé in Cameroon. After his stay in Bafia, he put himself into Zoa's hands "to learn and to serve". He went to live first at Nsimalen, a Canadian mission near Yaoundé. He contributed funds to improve the facilities of the leprosarium there as well as those of many other leprosaria in Africa.

At the time of the Cardinal's departure for Africa, people pictured him in the leper colonies where he'd originally planned to go. Even though most of his work was eventually with handicapped children, his contribution to the lepers was by no means negligible. We often forget that there are close to four million lepers in Africa; the Cardinal brought financial aid to eighty-two leper colonies in twenty African countries.

This aid took many forms: building huts to house the lepers, construction and outfitting of dispensaries, installation of running water and electricity. At Jamot, another leprosarium near Yaoundé, a small studio built with the help of gifts from the Cardinal gives lepers the chance to make a living by woodworking and by basket-weaving. "Work gives them a chance to regain the human dignity which they've lost," says Father Raymond Jaccard, one of the directors of the institution.

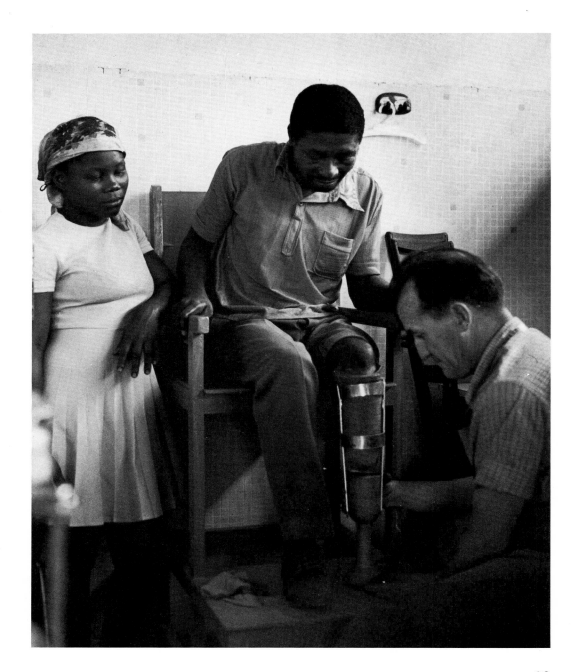

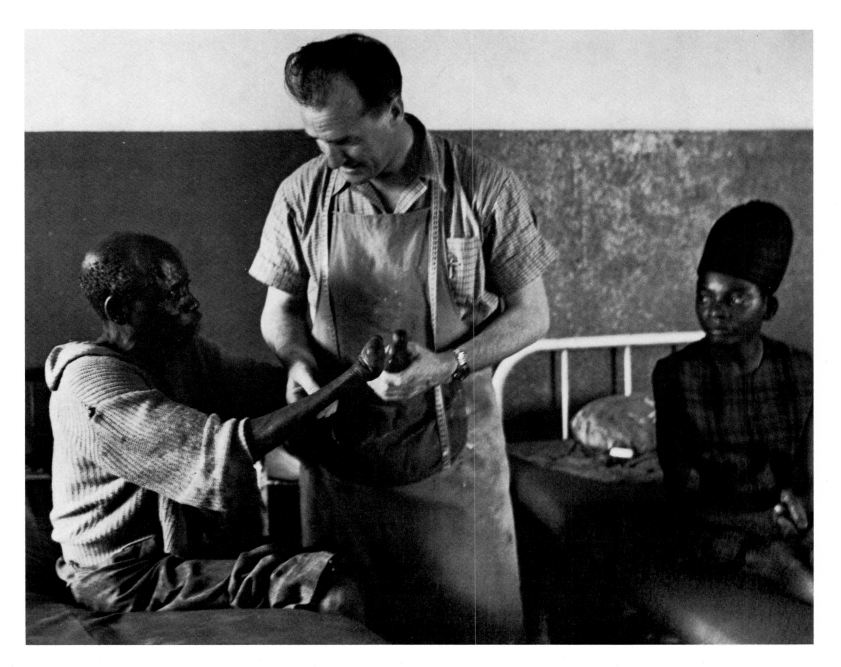

Raymond and Pierre Jaccard, both secular priests from France, are doing extraordinary work with the lepers; they make ingenious artificial limbs which allow the disabled to walk, work, and have an active life. It was wonderful to see the joy of Christine, a mother of seven who was trying an artificial leg for the first time. She was so enthusiastic about practising walking that she had to be stopped for fear she would become exhausted.

We now know how to stop the progress of leprosy, but in many cases, the sick are hesitant to ask for care. "In Africa, being a leper is almost a way of life," says Father Jaccard, "people who have the disease are taken care of by the State and no longer need to worry about making a living. That is why so many do not come for treatment until the last stages, when they're so ravaged by it that it is necessary to amputate an arm or leg. These people must be given a new reason for living. If we could form mobile teams of doctors and surgeons to go into the bush and treat the initial cases of leprosy, we could eliminate the disease in a few years," the priest added. But a project of this magnitude would demand such extensive planning that it couldn't be done except at the governmental level.

In Africa, a leprosarium resembles any other village, with its bamboo dwellings covered with clay, its roofs of palm leaves, chickens scratching in the dirt, and goats grazing between the huts. There is the same atmosphere, except that the inhabitants are missing a finger, a hand, a foot, or a leg.

In the village of Nbalmayo everyone was busy working when the Cardinal made an impromptu visit. When the Cardinal approached a leper doing some woodwork, the man did not at first recognize the visitor. The Cardinal came up to him, shook his hand, and asked him about his health. Suddenly the man realized to whom he was speaking and his face lit up and he cried: "You're the Cardinal! I've seen your

(Above) *Christine.* (Right) *Brothers Raymond and Pierre Jaccard fitting artificial limbs.*

photograph in the dispensary." And he announced the news to the whole village. People came out of all the huts, crying, "It's the Cardinal!" He was surrounded—everyone wanted to talk to him, to touch him. He shook their hands, kissed the children, and lavished words of encouragement.

The Cardinal looked discouraged as he left the village. "We can't help all the lepers," he said. "Our aid is like a drop of water in the ocean. One feels so helpless. The greatest danger is not of losing heart, but of saying to ourselves that we'll never see the end. We've barely finished one thing when we hear millions of other people calling. How can we respond to all these appeals?"

T HE CARDINAL has responded to numerous and varied appeals. In 1970, he founded a charitable corporation, called "Cardinal Léger and His Endeavours", whose purpose is to raise funds for the needs of developing nations and to administer and supervise the projects which he has undertaken. It receives funds and assistance from individuals, corporations, and foundations, and from government agencies and international organizations in Canada, the U.S. and Europe. To date, $4 million has been raised and spent on health and education facilities, public sanitation and economic development. Many African countries have benefited from these gifts. In Gabon, Dahomey, Nigeria, Ghana and Cameroon the money has funded the constructions of clinics, maternity hospitals, schools, residences for African priests and nuns, sanitation systems, leprosaria, social centres for reception and reorientation of juvenile delinquents, the rebuilding of hospitals, and academic scholarships for African students. Usually foreign governments administer distribution of food and programs of technical aid to the Third World. But the Cardinal considered the needs in the spheres of health and education to be just as urgent and therefore concentrated the greatest part of his efforts in these two areas.

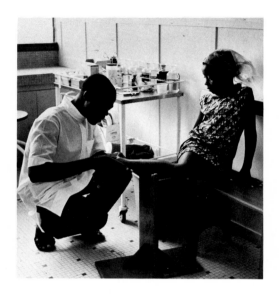

One may wonder why the Cardinal became so heavily involved with Africa's health problems, which take up 80 percent of his organization's budget. He explained this preoccupation when he received the Royal Bank of Canada Award in 1969, at which time he stressed that poverty, malnutrition, and disease characterized the countries of the Third World and that disease was most often aggravated by the first two problems. Poverty means lack of treatment, and undernourishment reduces resistance to disease. Africa's health needs are so great, its resources so inadequate, that without concrete aid, these countries couldn't possibly resolve the problems themselves. "The Third World is like a gigantic hospital waiting room," says the Cardinal. "The conse-

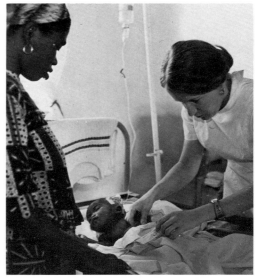

(Right) *Sister Lise Carignan has directed the Nsimalen dispensary for several years.*

quences of this situation are very grave; the repercussions are felt in the economic and social spheres since the productivity of these countries has been reduced by 30-60 percent." Thus, the Cardinal's efforts in the area of health care have enormous social repercussions. One of the central ideas behind the Cardinal's work is to give greater autonomy to as many as possible of the physically and mentally handicapped, and to help make these people active within their own milieu.

"The aid brought to the most neglected people of the Third World — the lepers, the sick, the mentally and physically disabled — has given me great comfort," he says. "To provide human beings with a way of participating in an active social life seems to me to be eminently worthwhile."

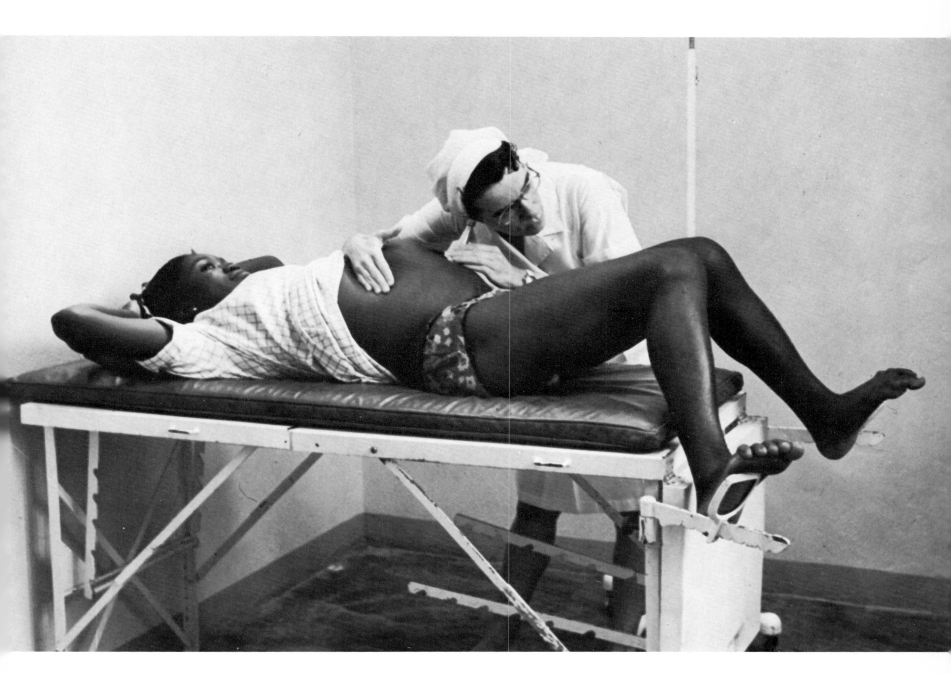

47

*Sister Claire Asselin, Order of St. Anne,
conducts a study session.*

49

AFTER LIVING FOR SOME TIME IN CAMEROON , the Cardinal had acquired a sensitive understanding of the area and had gotten to know the local authorities. He then decided to build a rehabilitation centre for the handicapped. "I didn't make a move without the consent of the local civil and religious authorities," he says. "Since coming here I have listened to the Africans and their leaders and I have learned a great deal from them. They are extremely open-minded and tolerant as long as we are responding to their real needs and not to what we imagine, rather superficially, to be their needs."

The Cardinal noted that the leprosaria are now quite well organized and run by government services or the missions. But another area, the care of handicapped children, had been completely ignored. Nearly 2 percent of the child population of Cameroon suffers from the after-effects of polio and the number of crippled children is shocking. In this tribal society, where sickness is accepted as an unavoidable calamity, the sick child is not rejected, but nothing is done to overcome his handicap. One often sees these young cripples dragging themselves along in the dirt amid general indifference. In some regions, these "reptile children" are even sacrificed to the "snake god". "No one is more vulnerable than a handicapped person in the Third World," affirms the Cardinal. He is very enthusiastic about his extremely useful project for the re-education of handicapped children.

The Cardinal obtained a beautiful piece of land from the Cameroonian government. It is on a hill overlooking the city of Yaoundé and was granted with the consent of the chiefs of the surrounding villages. The site was well chosen: the city is situated at the edge of a tropical forest on a series of hills about half a mile above sea level, and it is a region with a pleasant climate, warm and dry during the day and cool at night. The sunset, seen from the terrace of one of the Centre's pavilions, is a spectacular sight.

In this magnificent landscape, the Cardinal undertook the construction of the Centre. The Cameroonian government built an access road to the Centre and provided water and electrical services. During and after the construction, the Cardinal lived in a trailer at the edge of the site; this man, used to the comfortable life of a prelate, was content in a small lodging on the edge of the African bush. By living there, the Cardinal managed to avoid certain problems, among others the discord often provoked when gifts are made to underdeveloped countries.

It has very often happened that aid to underdeveloped countries does not really get to those to whom it was directed. By his presence, the Cardinal made sure that the donations were sent to the places of real need. "Those who come to Africa on a safari return with very superficial impressions," he says. "It is necessary to have lived with these people to be able to understand them."

Constructing the Centre

THE CENTRE FOR THE REHABILITATION OF THE HANDICAPPED at Yaoundé is composed of fourteen very functional buildings, well adapted to the climate and to the needs of the handicapped who are treated there. Overlooking the valley, surrounded by a garden of mimosas and bougainvilleas, the Centre looks very striking in this luxuriant landscape.

At the entrance is the dispensary where, from the early hours of the morning, patients come to wait on the benches outside. Many of them have walked miles since their last rest. They make use of the waiting time to exchange news, feed the baby, and picnic with the family. People come for treatment and advice, but they also come to make contact with a larger society than the one in their own village. A hundred people are seen in a day. They are treated mainly for malaria, parasites, and venereal diseases. Pregnant women and women with small children come for counselling. The more serious cases are referred to the hospital in Yaoundé.

Behind the dispensary is the main part of the Centre: the administration building, with a clerical staff composed entirely of Africans; the classrooms; the dormitories; the physiotherapy and occupational therapy rooms; and the prosthetics workshops. Children move through the covered hallways, some in wheelchairs, some leaning on crutches or wearing braces. Most of them are smiling—they take your hand, look for a caress or a little attention. Little Valentin has tears in his eyes: he's just arrived and is not used to being away from his mother. In a few days, he'll be as happy as the others. There are sixty boarders in the Centre and forty others who are brought in each day by bus; the number will likely double soon.

The physiotherapy rooms have equipment similar to that of Canadian rehabilitation hospitals, except for a special bed which can be raised gradually to a vertical position. Several of the small patients who

59

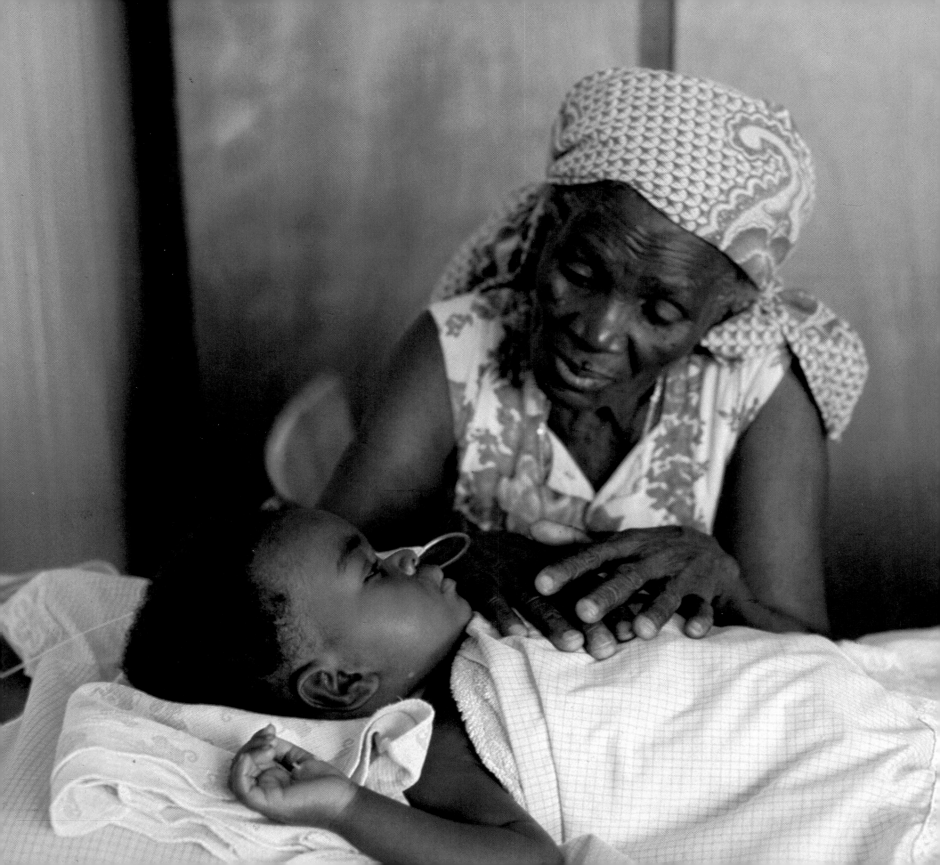

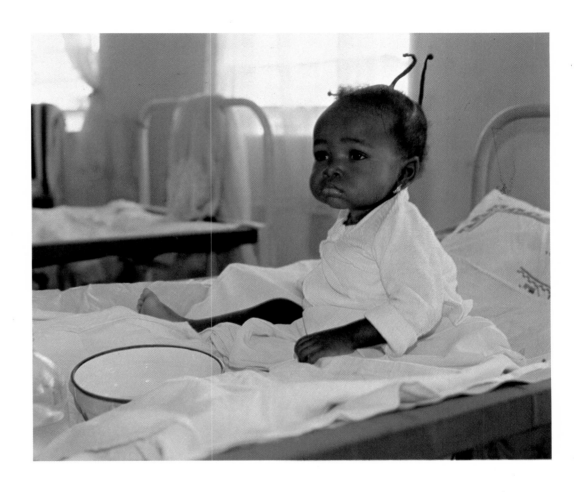

arrive at the Centre have lived all their lives in a horizontal position and their bodies could not bear being suddenly lifted upright; it must be done gently, each day gradually increasing the angle of the apparatus which supports them. Along the walls there are padded tables for kinestherapy. In a room adjacent are the whirlpool baths and hydrotherapy equipment. Among the children, all concentrating on exercises to help make them more self-reliant, the specialized staff go about their work good-humoredly. A Canadian physiotherapist teaches a mother how to do a massage which will give life to the paralyzed muscles of her child, so that when they return home, the mother can continue the treatment. Participation in the Centre's treatment gives the patients a sense of dignity; if people can't contribute funds, they contribute deeds.

After their daily treatment, the children go to school. A classroom like so many others awaits them: a blackboard, drawings tacked to the walls, the smell of chalk—only here one can attend a class while lying on a stretcher or sitting in a wheelchair. Oscar Njanga, the teacher, himself handicapped, moves among the children, helping them into more comfortable positions and constantly encouraging them. The atmosphere of this class is extraordinarily relaxed, and the children work happily. As a reward for his students' efforts, the teacher gets out his guitar and plays; they all sing and act or make up rhythms typical of African music.

Next door, in the prosthetics workshops, the craftsmen, some of whom are handicapped, work for the comfort of other handicapped persons. They take patients' measurements, cut and sew orthopedic shoes, invent support devices, make crutches. "This is probably the only place in the world where crutches are made out of mahogany!" proudly exclaims Maurice Nsamelu, one of the carpenters. Mahogany is common and cheap in Cameroon and the workers are ingenious at using local materials.

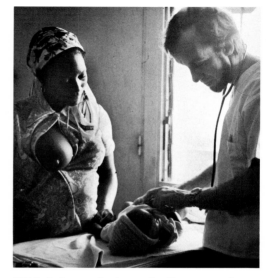

(Right) *A consultation at the dispensary. At the far end of the table is Doris Albert, a nurse who has worked at the Centre for two years.*

62

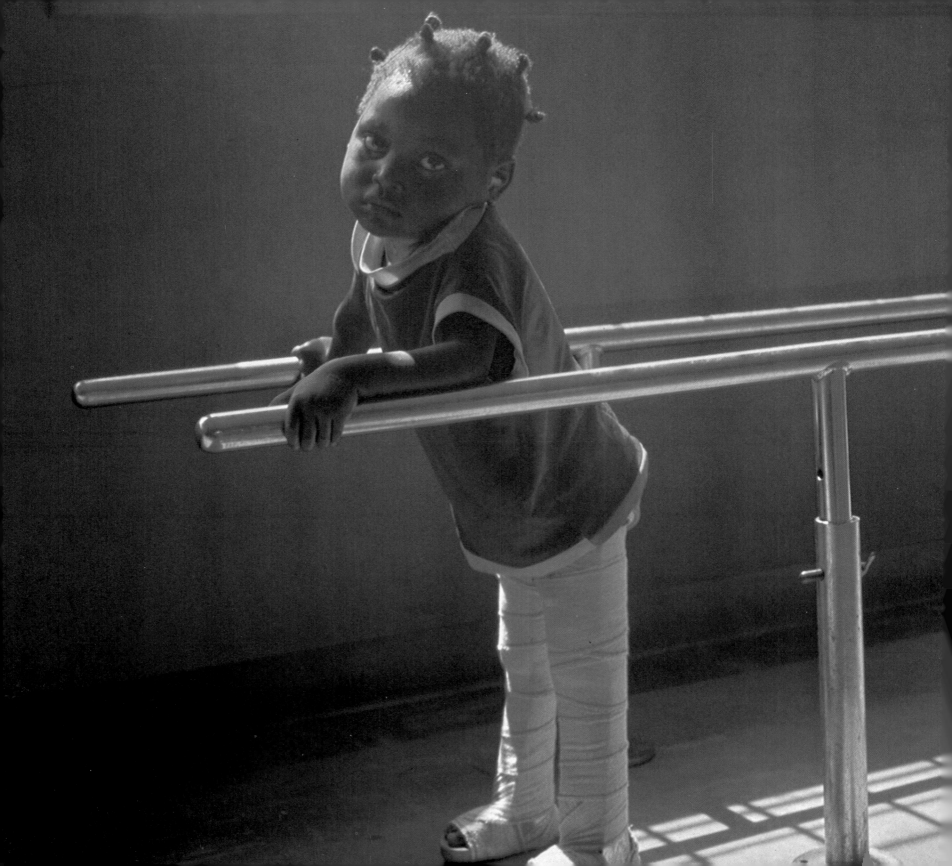

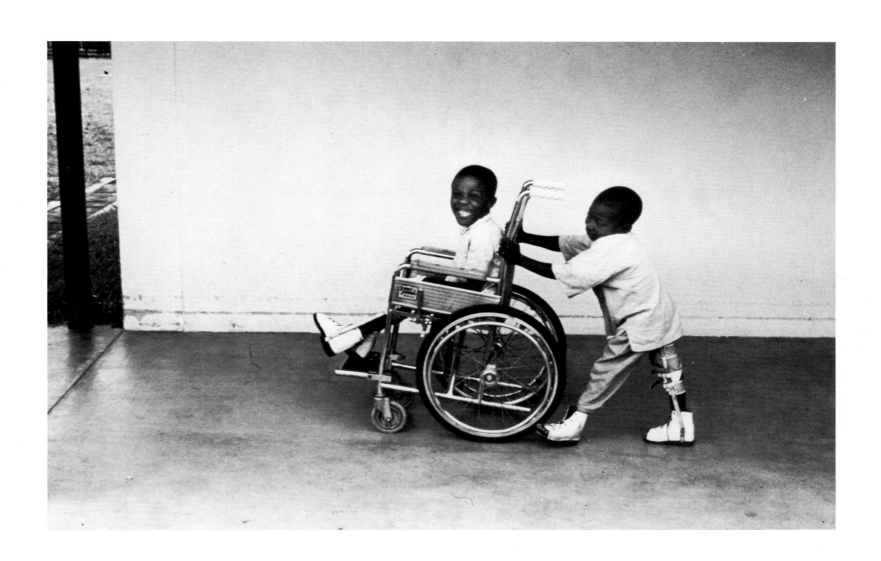

Charitable donations are often made without much thought, as is shown in a gift of thirty Canadian-made wheelchairs sent to the Centre from a Canadian institution. The chairs were usable in the interior of the institution, where the cement walks were smooth and even, but if the children wanted to take them outside the Centre, the chairs couldn't stand up to the jolts caused by the rough African roads. It was expensive and difficult to get parts from Canada, so the craftsmen simply reconstructed the chairs, using the frames and adding bicycle parts and a solid structure of their own invention. The artisans' refabrication cost only $40 each whereas the Canadian ones had cost $500. In addition, repairs were made quickly and without much expense.

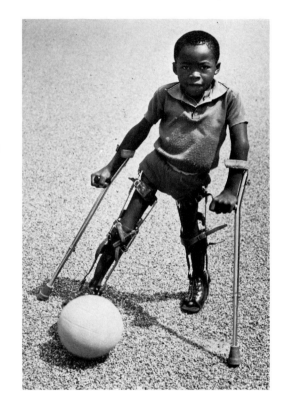

Farther on is the occupational therapy room. Young women, several of whom are handicapped, teach the children the rudiments of weaving, basket making, and sewing. The very young children express themselves by drawing, and their work is touching in its universality of expression which goes far beyond living conditions, climate, and race.

At mealtime, all of the small community is in the dining room where a healthy meal helps them regain their energy. They sing while waiting to be served; it seems that music and chanting come as naturally to them as breathing. "The African seems to have a sort of biological joy," says the Cardinal. "In the worst situations, he still finds something to laugh or sing about." The menu is made up of local dishes: rice, chicken, zebu (an ox-like domestic animal), pork, vegetables such as sweet potato and avocado, and fruit—papayas, bananas, and oranges. The children are not lacking in appetite; in fact they are benefiting from a diet which follows the principles of good nutrition and is probably better balanced than the one they have at home.

The Centre takes care of all children who come, no matter their language or religion. Some even come from neighboring countries such as Chad and Gabon. The language spoken at the Centre is French but

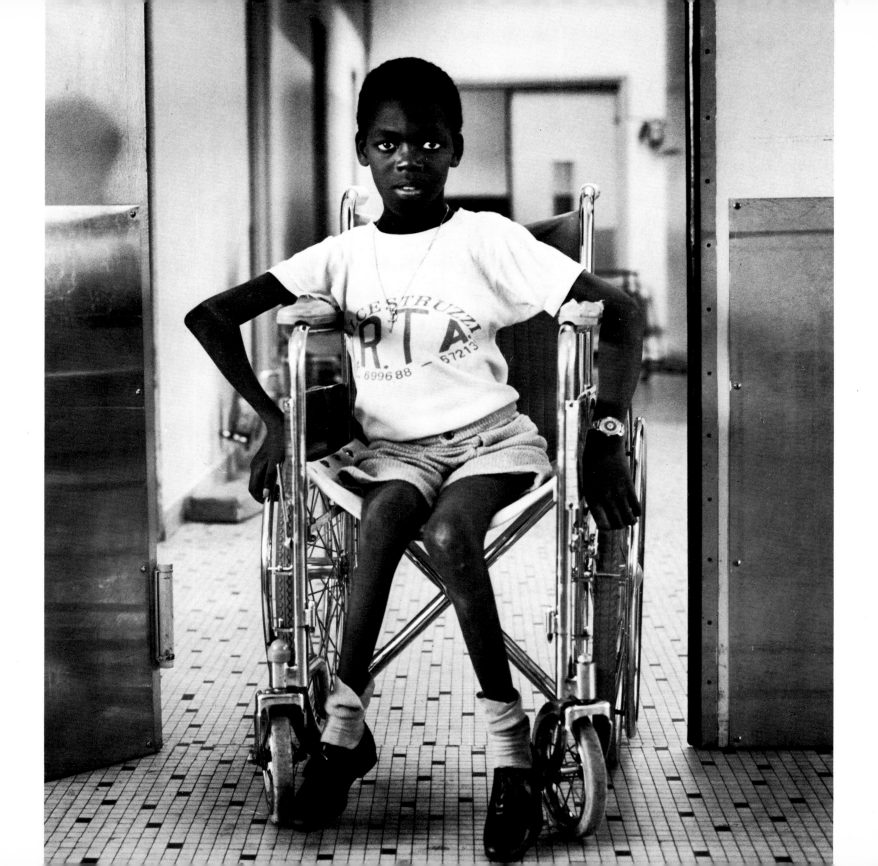

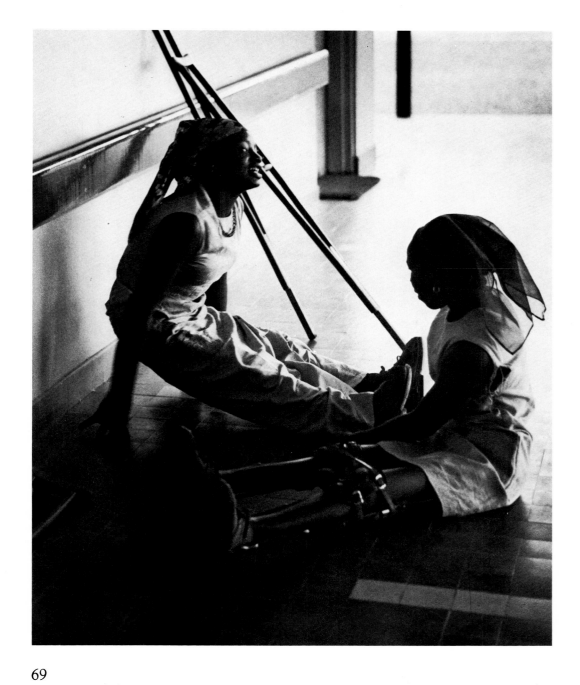

the staff can get along in several dialects and they occasionally use interpreters. The predominant religion is Roman Catholic, but there seems to be no pressure on the part of the administration to impose religious practice.

"I believe that what we must bring the people here is not complicated theology, but the witness of a life consecrated to God. Such a life is not a series of extraordinary events, but simply loving attention to the needs of others."

One Sunday we observed the children going to the chapel as if going to a party. They were so overjoyed by the event that the monitors had to restrain some of their enthusiasm. It must be added that this was a day when the Cardinal was saying Mass and that when the Cardinal is present, there is always rejoicing.

Although priority is given to children, adults are occasionally treated at the Centre: for example, Jean Essomba, the chief of a neighboring village, was a polio victim when he was very young and had never walked in his life. At fifty-eight, this man has a new life, thanks to the walking apparatus and crutches the Centre made for him. Every day he is brought in by car, and with a smile which shows his pleasure at finally being able to move by himself, he does his exercises faithfully.

The children stay at the Centre for six months to one year. The medical directors of the Centre are trying to reduce this stay to a minimum so as not to keep the children too long from their home surroundings. Several years ago, with the best intentions in the world, some children were sent to European hospitals, but after a few years, it was very difficult to reintegrate them into their old way of life. Now they are trying to reduce the child's stay at the institution as much as possible. They accept only those children for whom they can do something under the rehabilitation program, and 85 percent of their patients learn how to walk again. For the time being, priority is given to polio

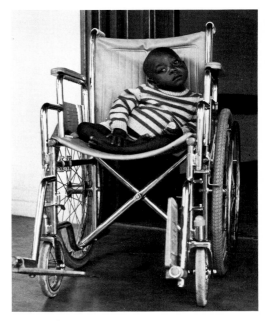

Little Valentin

70

Hydrotherapy

73

victims, but eventually, they would like to give equal attention to adults and to all the other handicapped, whatever the origin of their problem. At the moment, it's necessary to concentrate on treating the ones who need it most.

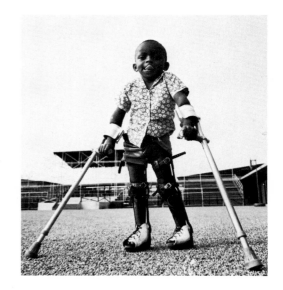

The Centre is already treating mentally handicapped children. The Cardinal had three buildings constructed adjacent to the Centre, which he then turned over to the association of the parents of the handicapped children. The association, composed entirely of Cameroonian parents, set up a treatment and teaching centre for mentally retarded children in the area, which was poetically named "La Colombe" (The Dove). Opened in 1972, La Colombe looks after children five to sixteen years of age who are mentally retarded, have emotional or personality problems, or problems in school. A German specialist, Gisela Kraetzch, directs the Centre and is assisted by two other specialists and five teachers. Forty children attend the school and each is given individual attention. One of Dr. Kraetzch's favorite methods is play therapy, which has produced excellent results with disturbed children. The plastic arts, music, and dance give the children a way of expressing themselves, and they are also taught a minimum program of basic school subjects. The whole group is picked up and taken home by bus every day. Though the school is administered entirely by Cameroonians, it continues to receive financial aid from the Cardinal's organization.

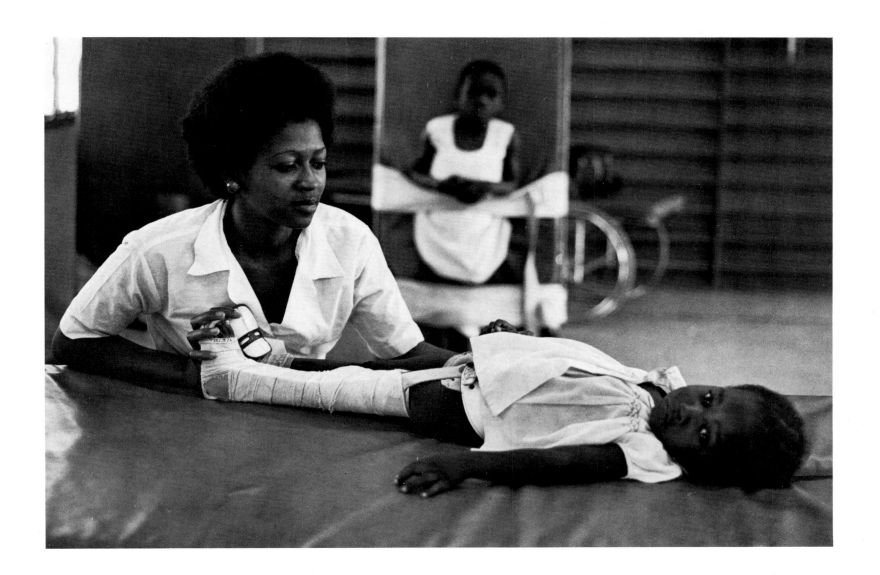

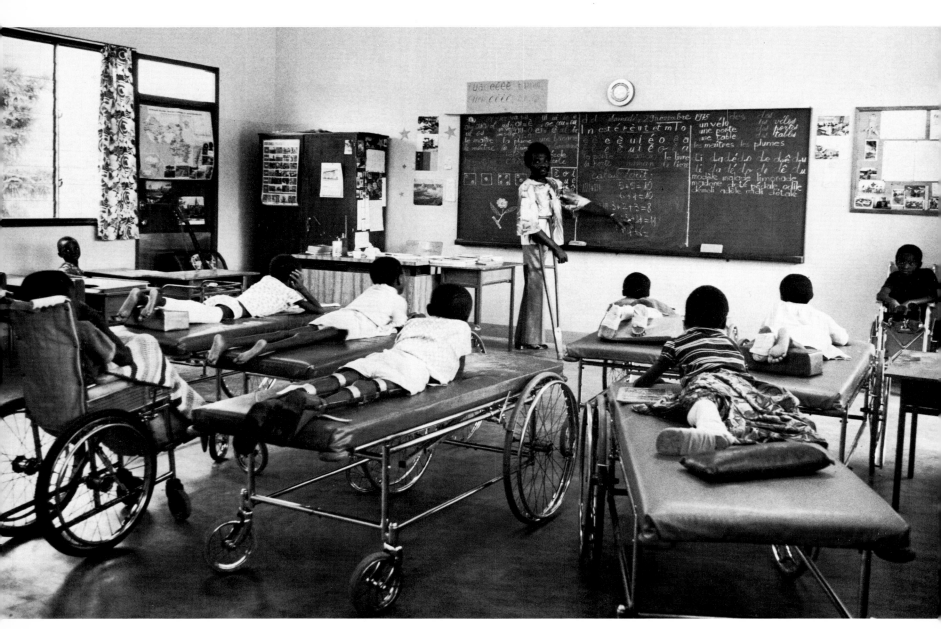

Oscar Njanga

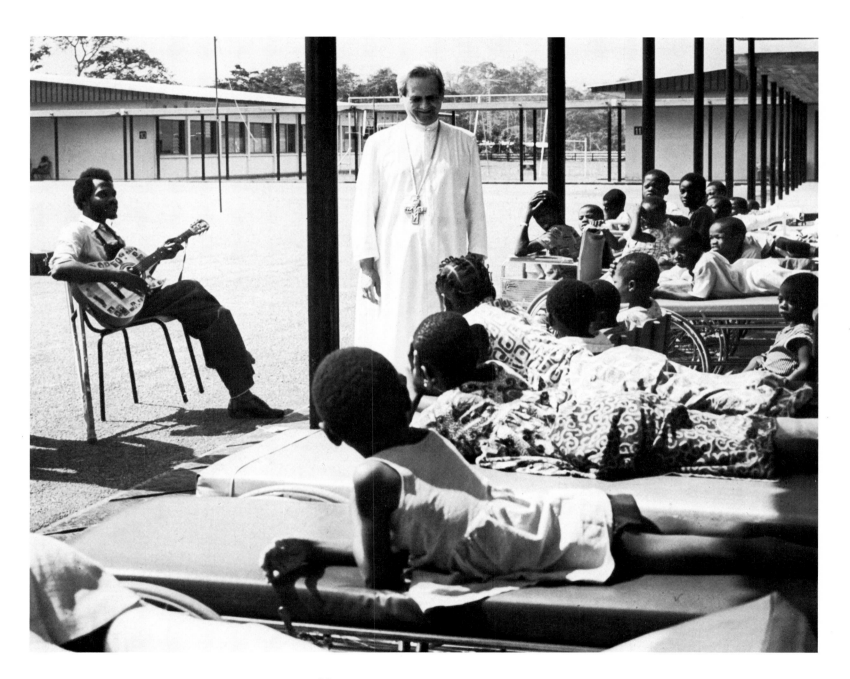

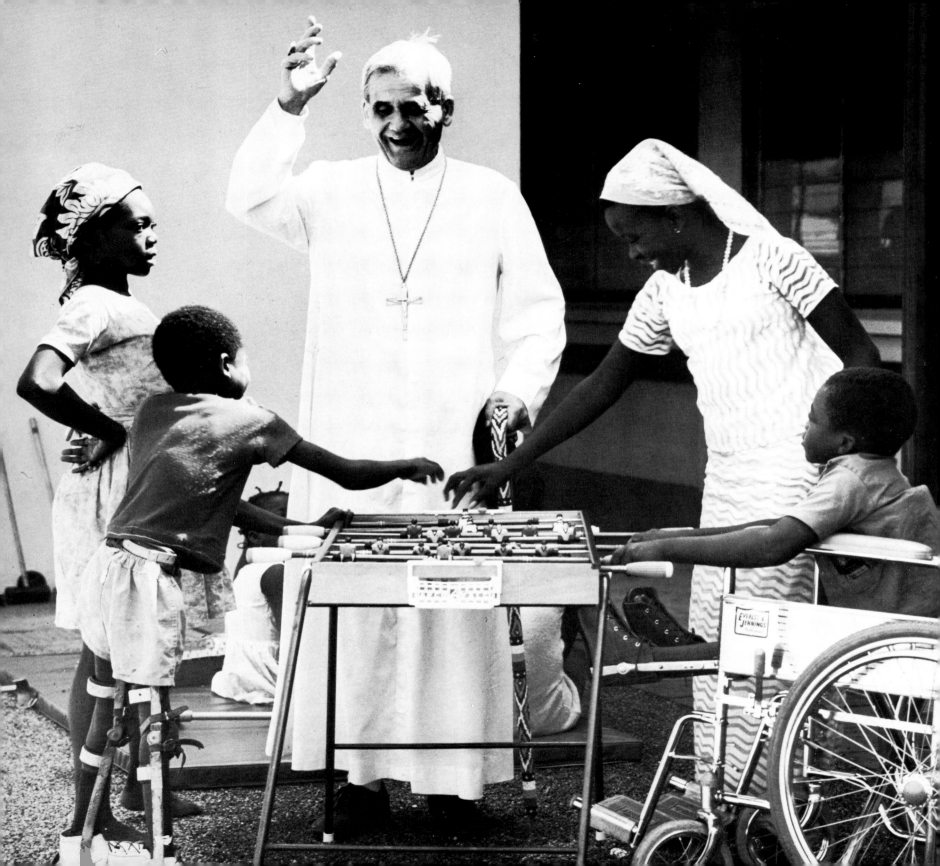

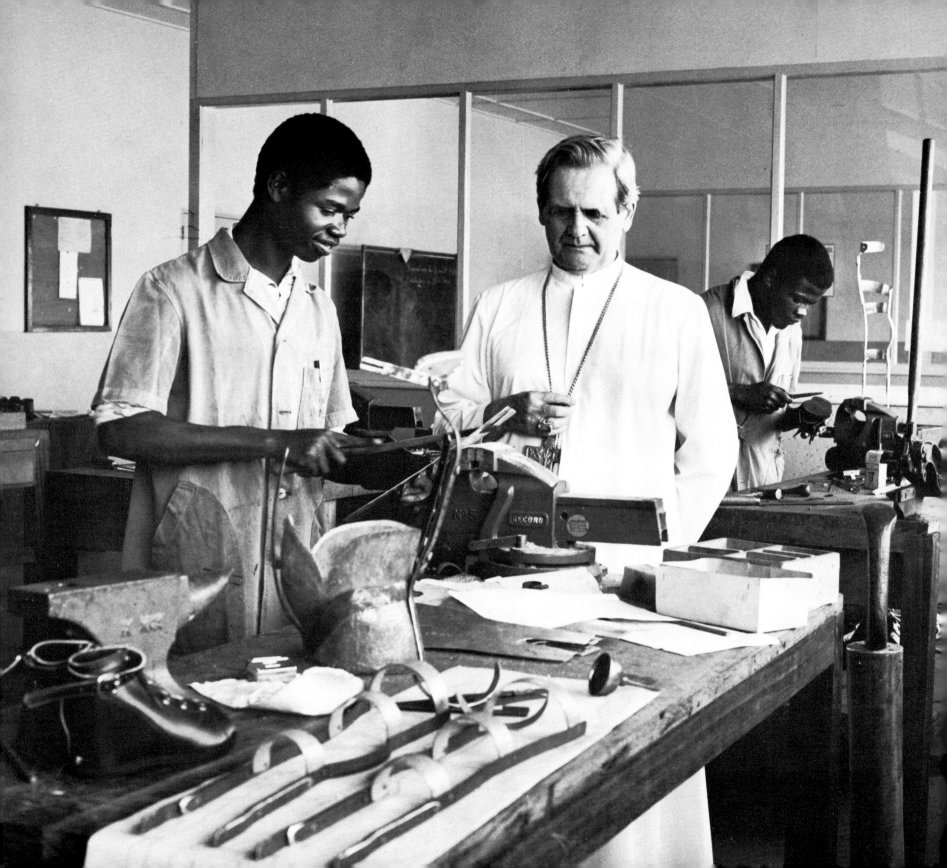

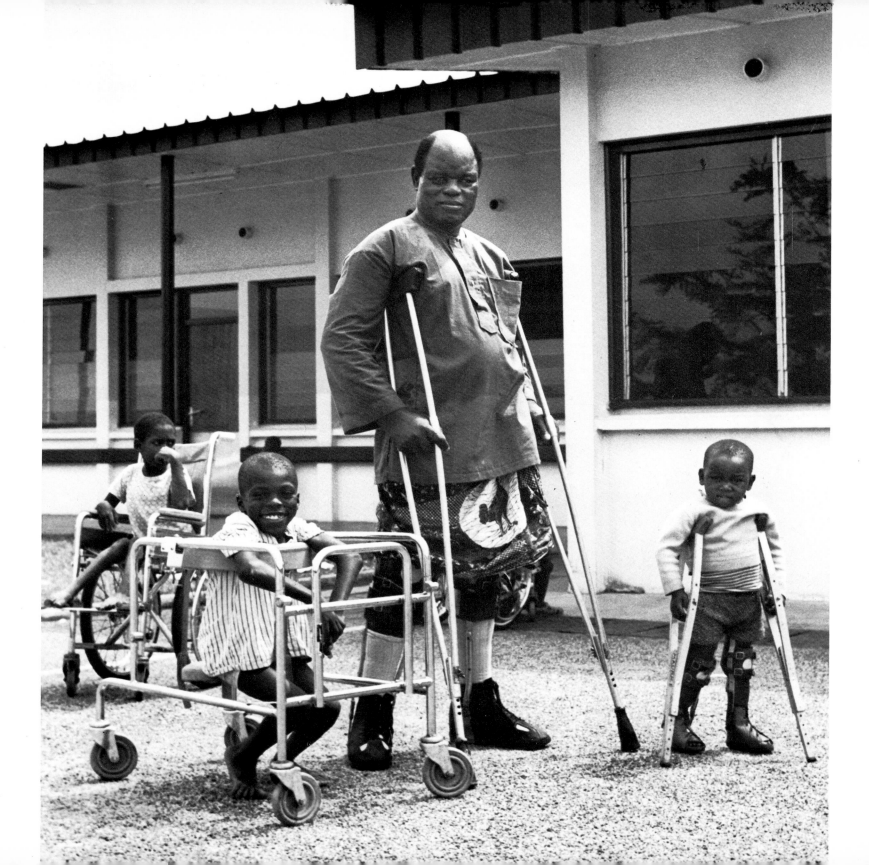

(Above) *Madeleine herself is handicapped. She
has been at the Centre since its opening and is
in charge of occupational therapy.* (Left) *Chief
Jean Essomba*

95

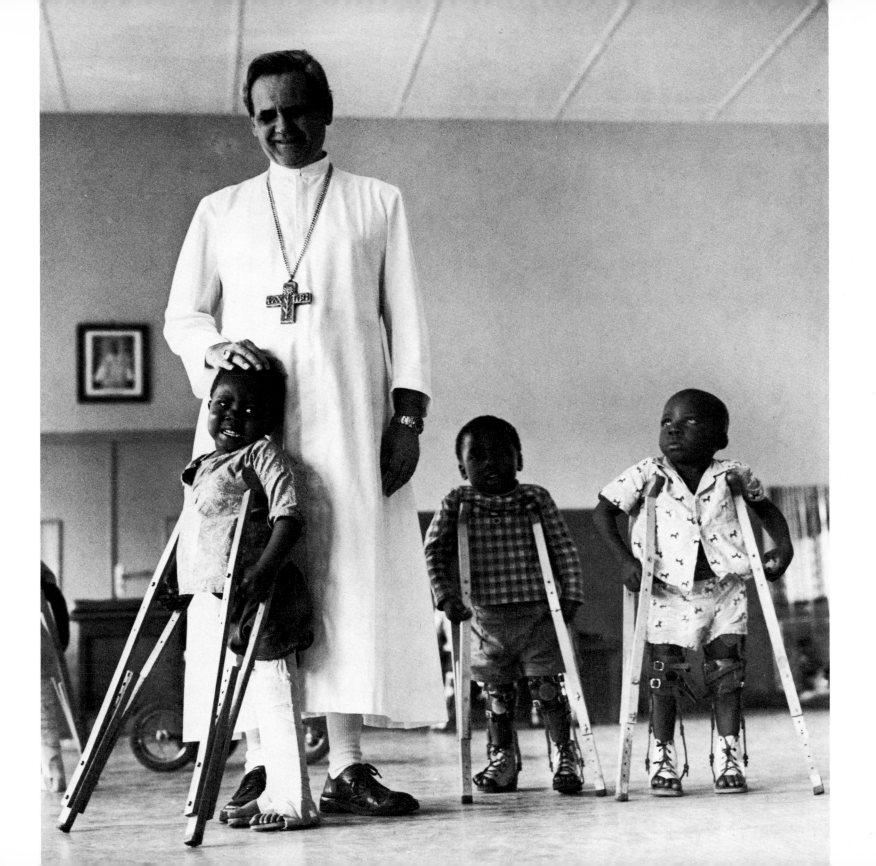

Doctor Gisela Kraetzch

Miss Ilonka Lessnau helping a student in her art class

103

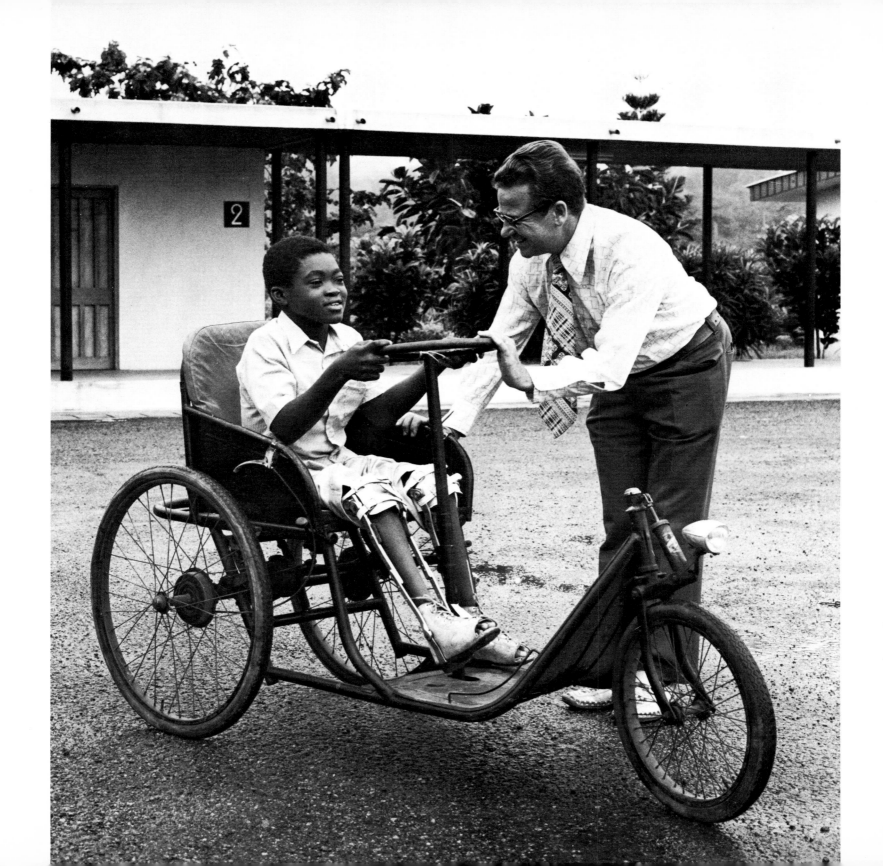

THE CENTRE has a social service bureau which is directed by Brother Camille Dugré, who works as the liaison between the institution and the family environment. Brother Dugré has lived in Africa for twenty years and is very familiar with the African scene. He speaks several local dialects and a little "pidgin", which allows him to communicate with the people quite well. (There are about 100 tribes and as many dialects.) He arranges to take the children home when their stay at the Centre is over and he sees to the integration of the young person back into his family.

One day Jean Minka, a small boy of ten, was going home after being equipped with braces and adjustable crutches which helped him to walk almost normally. His mother had made a long trip to come and get him, so Brother Dugré set off in the morning to drive her and the boy back to their village about eighty miles away. But he hadn't counted on the hazards of the African climate. The rainy season was officially over but it had rained in one area, with the result that the car constantly got stuck in the mud and had to be pushed out with the help of passers-by. Brother Dugré, covered with mud from head to toe, finally had to leave Jean and his mother with some friends. The police were given the responsibility of taking the small family home once the roads were in better condition. As for Brother Dugré, it was only another adventure in a job which is never monotonous.

(Above) *President Ahmadou Ahidjo of Cameroon with the Cardinal at the Centre's opening, January 1972.* (Left) *The Cardinal and Monsignor Etoga, Bishop of M'Balmayo, and Dr. Victor Goldbloom* (Centre)

THE CENTRE FOR THE REHABILITATION OF THE HANDICAPPED at Yaoundé is the Cardinal's most ambitious project and the one which he holds dearest to his heart. It was designed by a Swiss architect, C. H. Strobel, and the construction was done by the Gecicam Company (Engineering and Construction of Cameroon). The Centre is very functional and well adapted to the climate, with its covered hallways where the children can move about freely during the rainy season. The dining halls and classrooms have plenty of room for handling wheelchairs and stretchers. "When I visited the site for the first time," says the Cardinal, "the hill was covered with thorn bushes and anteaters . . . " You'd have to see the anteaters, which can grow almost to the size of a man, and the entanglement of the bush, to understand the Cardinal's pride as he views the Centre's handsome exterior today, surrounded by gardens and lawns.

The construction, equipment and expenses of the Centre represent an investment of about $2.5 million, of which $1.5 million was furnished by the "Cardinal and His Endeavours". The Canadian government contributed close to $1 million. "Without the help of Canadians, the Centre would never have seen the light of day," says the Cardinal. The Cameroonian government provided the land, a modern access road and water and electrical services, but in the beginning they were unable to finance the operation of the Centre.

In spite of many problems, the project received unanimous approval. The Centre was officially opened on January 15, 1972 in the presence of the president of Cameroon, Ahmadou Ahidjo, Canadian cabinet ministers Jean Chrétien and Victor Goldbloom, the Papal Delegate and about 400 Canadians.

Even though the Centre depends mainly on donations, and though most of the families who send their children there are very poor, they are asked to contribute something to the cost of their child's treatment.

(Above) *Canadian Cabinet Minister Jean Chrétien with the Cardinal at the opening ceremony*

Even if the contribution is nominal, it is requested in order to maintain the dignity of those who benefit from the Centre, and also to help lead these people, who previously have received aid without being consulted, towards a healthy autonomy. In this agricultural economy, gifts of produce are often accepted, and it is not unusual to receive a sheep or a goat in payment.

Nevertheless, the local population contributes only a small percentage of the cost of running the Centre. The care of each young patient costs about $1,500 per year. International organizations, such as the Swiss "Terre des Hommes" organization, sponsor thirty of the children, and sixteen others have Canadian sponsors who pay the entire cost of their treatment. Cardinal Léger and His Endeavours must find the balance of the funds necessary to maintain and develop the Centre, which has an annual budget of over a half million dollars. When the Canadian Minister of External Affairs, Allan MacEachen, visited in April 1975, the Centre was given assurance that from 1977 on, the Canadian government will contribute to the cost of maintenance, and for its part, the Cameroonian government is prepared to pay 25 percent of the costs from the same date. This last contribution is in keeping with the general policy of gradually handing over the Centre to the local authorities.

Always carefully overseeing the growth and development of his work, the Cardinal planned from the beginning to turn over the Centre to the Africans. Of a staff of 100 people, there are now only 10 Canadian and European employees. One Cameroonian doctor, Dr. Isaac Ebengué, is studying at the Institute of Rehabilitation in Montreal under the director, Dr. Gustave Gingras, himself one of the consultants for the Yaoundé Centre. A physiotherapy professor, Louise Brisette of Laval University, is training African physiotherapists. In the administration, the members of the office staff are preparing to take over under the able direction of Gaspard Massue and Rollande Dominique.

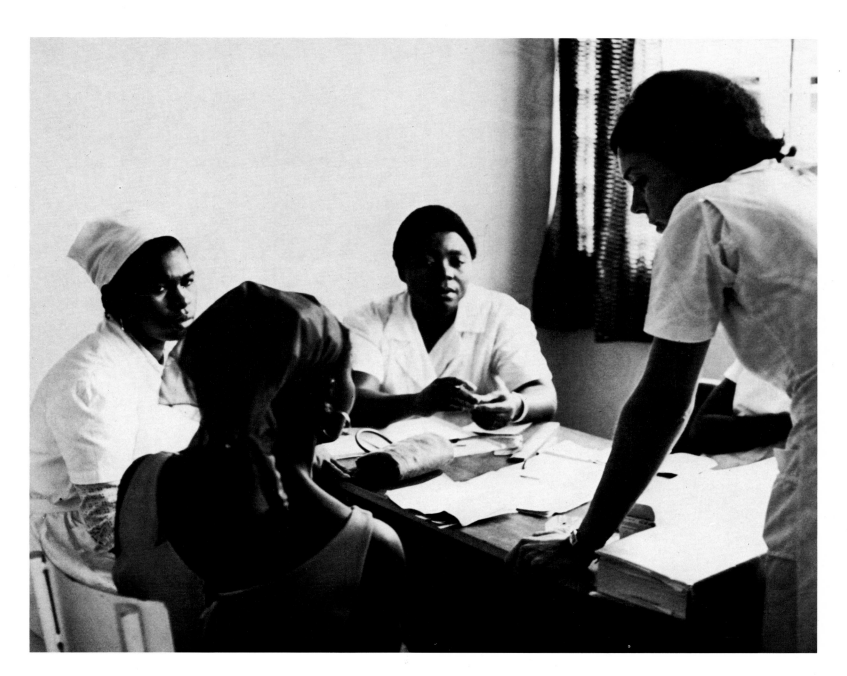

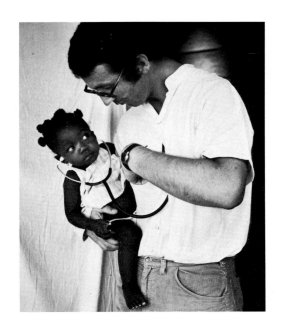

Dr. Gustave Gingras has acquired a world-wide reputation in the area of rehabilitation and has leant his considerable talents as consultant to the directors of the Centre. According to him, one of the reasons for the success of the project comes from the fact that because it is known that Canada has never been a colonial power, Canadians are welcomed in the African milieu. "Canadians have become the real missionaries of health in Africa," he says. Dr. Gingras believes that even when an African staff finally takes over, Canadians will continue to play an important role, mainly in terms of training staff and providing financial support.

THE PEOPLE

(Left) *A visit with the village elder*

T O UNDERSTAND the Cardinal's work, we must see it in its African context.

In the Yaoundé area the earth is red and the walls of the houses are made from red clay brick. In this part of the country, the dead are often buried in front of their homes; the little hut surrounded by its small garden and tombs is symbolic of the cycle of man living on the earth and returning to it. Around the dwellings, which are scattered in no particular order, and on the roads, or rather on the paths as they are called here, chickens, pigs, and goats wander freely. In the midst of this activity, dozens of semi-nude children play or crawl in the dust — it's no wonder that they are infected by parasites. The adults, dressed in brightly colored clothes, sit on the ground to talk because furniture is rare. Women and children carry heavy loads on their heads; cans of water taken from the public fountain and piles of bananas bought in the market are two common examples. The market is really a gathering of people at a crossroads. Merchants simply set up shop on the ground or form a pyramid of oranges or papayas on their mats, spread out a bag of peanuts, put a few cooked pancakes on the charcoal, and sit in the sun, waiting for a customer. Many take shelter under umbrellas which serve as sun-shades.

Everyone walks in Africa because other methods of transport are rare. The roads are covered with people who amble along nonchalantly. The women, besides carrying their babies on their backs, usually have some other load on their heads, and children carry school books in the same manner. It's an amusing scene to watch the students leaving school: as everywhere, they come out of school running and playing, but their books stay balanced on their heads.

In spite of the comparatively primitive way of life, everyone seems to be in good humor. As you stroll along the road, you never stop smiling and saying hello. "When the African has cried for eight hours,

119

he will laugh for the next eight," says the Cardinal. "He exorcizes his trouble by joyous laughter and exuberant dancing." This is true of most Africans living in the bush; those in the cities and towns are more reserved.

Cameroon is part of West Africa, situated on the Atlantic coast near the equator, and is a country endowed with a varied terrain. In the north there is the savanna; in the centre, mountains; and in the south, tropical forest. The population is almost six million. The two largest cities, Douala and Yaoundé, are quite different. Situated on the coast in a low, humid terrain, the port of Douala is a bustling commercial and industrial city like many other African metropolitan centres. Yaoundé, the "city of seven hills" is the administrative and intellectual capital; hotels, government buildings, and residences surrounded by gardens make the centre of the city very attractive. It was in the suburbs of this pleasant capital that the Cardinal established his headquarters.

Strangely enough, Cameroon has a linguistic situation similar to that of Canada. Prior to 1914, the country was called German West Africa, but at the end of the war it was divided into British and French protectorates. In the federal union formed in 1961, the French element predominates. It has one of the best school attendance records in Africa, with 80 percent of the children going to school; however, the rate of illiteracy is still very high among adults. More than 10,000 students attend university in Cameroon.

The people in Cameroon live on very little; the annual per capita income is only about $160. The country has few industries, the most important of which are aluminium smelters and electrical generating stations. Most of the people in Cameroon make a living from agriculture, the main crops being coffee, cocoa, cotton, and bananas. There are a few large plantations but most are small ones cleared from the forest. The traditional division of labor still exists: "This country rests on the

122

(Above) *This boy routinely walks more than ten miles to market with a heavy load balanced on his head.*

shoulders of women," remarks the Cardinal, "it is they who do most of the farming, still carrying their children on their backs."

Cameroon has been independent since 1960 and became a federal republic in 1961. The president of the republic, Ahmadou Ahidjo, is a Moslem from the north of the country and he proudly wears a djellaba and a fez. He has great admiration for the humanity and understanding that Cardinal Léger has shown in his work in Cameroon. Since he officially opened the Centre for the Handicapped, the president has continued to take an interest in its progress. The relations between the Cardinal and government authorities are excellent, because he has demonstrated his knowledge of how to respond adequately to the needs of a Third World country.

The Centre filled a void in the Cameroonian hospital system. As elsewhere in Africa, health services are extremely inadequate—Cameroon has only 225 doctors for a population of almost six million. There are about forty hospitals, but most of them are really dispensaries and very poorly equipped.

It is no wonder that polio has made such ravages. In conjunction with the movement for the rehabilitation of the handicapped undertaken by the Cardinal, a major campaign has been organized for the prevention of polio. Canada has provided huge quantities of vaccine, and all over the country, posters invite the population to be vaccinated. But the problems of transportation, lack of refrigeration, and local attitudes all hinder the success of these precautions, and progress is very slow. At the Centre they're far from being able to deal with all the demands.

But the Centre at Yaoundé exists and functions, and it will continue to improve. The construction of the Centre has even had unforeseen effects; the surrounding area has become quite well developed and the neighboring villages profit from the comings and goings of people

127

around the institution. A market has been set up at the crossroads. All along the road, huts are being built and transformed into little stands, pretentiously called "cafés", where beer and soft drinks are sold. There is even a café in the area of the Centre which proclaims proudly, "Centre for the Handicapped Café".

Cotton is spun into cloth for the use of the local tailor.

137

(Left) *Mass at Yaoundé*

(Left) *Pigmy school children with wooden writing boards*

A Pygmy family

153

A village in northern Cameroon

157

161

175

178

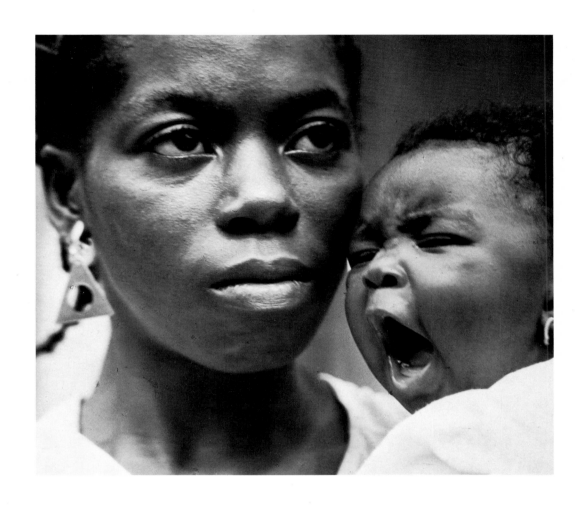

185

(Above) *On behalf of Variety Clubs International, Danny Kaye presents the Cardinal with the Humanitarian of the Year Award.*

THERE IS NO DOUBT that the projects which the Cardinal has started in Africa are well established and provide a great service. But they will need to be continually supplemented, even when they are operated entirely by Africans. In spite of the success of the projects already completed, the Cardinal is not satisfied. He plans to start a technical school to teach trades to the handicapped and he wants to help the orphans, the old people, and the delinquents, all of whom are neglected. "We have exported our way of life to Africa, but we have also exported other effects of urbanization and industrialization: juvenile delinquency, the neglect of orphans and the elderly. We have profited from the resources of these countries, now we must correct the social consequences of our intervention." The Cardinal does not solicit money in the name of charity, but in the name of social conscience. Our contribution to reducing the inequalities between ourselves and the people of the Third World is not a matter of charity, but of justice. "We whites have responsibilities to the black continent. Almost impossible obstacles separate us from these people because instinctively, they think of the slavery of which they've been victims, of colonialism, and a certain neocolonialism. We are the symbols of that past reality."

The Cardinal has taken on the job of attracting public and governmental attention to the problems of the Third World and he uses his prestige to establish a bridge between the poor and the rich. Often, we feel totally helpless in confronting the immense poverty of a large part of the world; fortunately there are a few men such as the Cardinal, through whom aid can be channelled.

The Cardinal received the Royal Bank of Canada Award in 1969. The recognition brought by this award and the donations which came to him provided the impetus for the formation of his organization. The president of Cameroon, Ahmadou Ahidjo, has given him the country's

highest decoration, the Commander's Medal of the Order of Bravery. The Variety Club, an international charitable organization of showbusiness people, presented Cardinal Léger with the Variety Clubs International Humanitarian Award for 1975 for his work with crippled children, an honor which includes a substantial donation. Past recipients of this award include Winston Churchill, Martin Luther King, Albert Schweitzer, and Dr. Salk. The Cardinal accepts all these honors very humbly.

The achievements of the Cardinal were not obtained without a great deal of anguish. There were many obstacles to overcome in carrying out his projects. The administrative problems, difficult under the best circumstances, were compounded by the differences in language, background and outlook of North Americans, Africans and Europeans; by the climate, and the susceptibility of Westerners to local maladies; and by the distance between the Cardinal and his Montreal office. To succeed, persistence alone was not sufficient; faith was also required.

A man who has achieved so much in a full career must have many satisfying memories. But the Cardinal is not given to passive reminiscence. "I take what the Lord gives me from day to day. I don't encumber myself with memories — very often, memories paralyze action. I strive only to make the Gospel not seem a lie."

The Cardinal believes that the central issue of our times comes down to the recognition that, though man is an individual, he can only be redeemed through the responsible community of the global village. Each of us is part of humanity. The path to peace must be built on respect for the dignity and equality of all people, regardless of their economic situation. By his example, he has shown us how to reach out to the disadvantaged of the world. He reminds us that "the first mission of life calls us to look into our own hearts and then ask, 'What can I do'?"